Wc
Ph

Pionee .ᴜᴜᴜ

Women Photographers

Pioneers 1851–1936

Introduction and biographies
by Clara Bouveresse

Photofile

The Photofile series is the original English-language edition of the Photo Poche collection. It was first published between 1986 and 1992 by the Centre National de la Photographie, Paris, with the support of the French Ministry of Culture. Robert Delpire (1926–2017) was the creator of the series and its managing editor until 2017. The general editor of this volume was Sarah Moon.

Translated from the French *Femmes photographes: L'ouverture des possibles* by Francisca Garvie

Cover design and typesetting by Matthew Young

First published in the United Kingdom in 2020 by Thames & Hudson Ltd, 181A High Holborn, London WC1V 7QX

www.thamesandhudson.com

Original edition © 2020 Actes Sud, France
This edition © 2020 Thames & Hudson Ltd, London

British Library Cataloguing-in-Publication Data
A catalogue record for this book is available from the British Library

ISBN 978-0-500-41115-5

Printed and bound in Italy

To find out about all our publications, please visit **www.thamesandhudson.com**. There you can subscribe to our e-newsletter, browse or download our current catalogue, and buy any titles that are in print.

Foreword

The publisher Robert Delpire launched the Photo Poche collection
in 1982. Published in English as the Photofile series, they were
designed to be pocket-sized reference works at affordable prices.
Of the 159 titles published in French since the series began,
more than a hundred are monographs on men, as opposed to
a dozen or so on women, although women also appear in some
anthologies and works devoted to specific subjects. This situation
reflected an ongoing lack of recognition of women photographers
by photographic institutions and the art market. Most of the big
names that appeared in exhibitions and books were men, and for
a long time, scant attention was paid to women or to non-Western
photographers. From 2010 onwards, the situation began to change
radically, thanks to a number of collective initiatives and
major exhibitions.

    Aware of these disparities, Robert Delpire wanted to devote
a three-volume boxed set to women photographers. He had been
impressed by the documentary *Objectif femmes*, directed by Manuelle
Blanc and Julie Martinovic and produced by Sylvie Gauthier. After
Delpire's death, the project was continued by his wife, photographer
Sarah Moon, and by the archivist Odile Pütz, with support from
Michel Poivert, a professor of art history and photography.

    From the outset, Robert Delpire's aim in this project was to
represent each photographer with a single selected image and a
brief biography. The result is three volumes devoted to women
photographers in chronological order. This initiative is not

intended to compensate for earlier deficiencies but is meant to stand alongside future monographs on women photographers. It represents a first step – no doubt it is not enough, but it is nonetheless necessary. The photographers included here were not selected on the grounds that they took a supposedly 'female' approach but simply because they have been ignored for too long. The three volumes in this set try to take a broad view of the history of photography, in all its richness and variety, by looking at the specific approaches taken by each of these women.

This first volume begins with a dedication to the many 'anonymous' women photographers who do not appear in these three volumes. The image selection reflects the situation as it was in the late 2010s. By that time, a number of women photographers had become better known and even widely renowned, featuring in exhibitions and catalogues and included in museum collections. Others still remain in the shadows, however, their archives scattered, but we hope they will be included in future editions as and when they are rediscovered. We have tried to showcase the huge diversity of works produced by women photographers, ranging from photojournalism to studio portraits, fashion photography, photomontage and commercial photography, both in black and white and in colour. We have included women photographers from all over the world, although the West predominates, yet again because women there are currently better integrated into the public arenas of art and photography. Some artists whose work extends beyond the framework of photography into realms including performance and installation art, like Barbara Kruger and Hannah Wilke, are not featured here, although the borders between these art forms remain fluid. The format of this series imposes an additional constraint: it includes just one image per photographer, which is by its nature a partisan choice, and gives precedence to vertical or square photographs because they are better suited to the size and shape of these volumes. So the selection is necessarily fragmentary and deserves to be revised and extended. Yet this foundation stone in the history of women photographers is nonetheless a valuable contribution, even if it is not a definitive survey. It is an invitation to discover women photographers, until the day comes when, as we hope, there will be no more need for such initiatives. The choice of photographs reflects our subjective taste: these are images that struck, surprised or moved us and we hope they will also intrigue and awaken the curiosity of all readers who love photography.

Clara Bouveresse is a historian of photography, who wrote the introductions and biographies for these volumes and aided Sarah Moon and Odile Pütz with the selection of photographs.

Paving the Way

Women began using cameras from the moment they were invented and continued to practise photography throughout the second half of the 19th century, at a time when it was still a new, experimental and constantly evolving art form. In that period, when the emerging profession was not yet subject to any codes or rules, women were free to immerse themselves in photography. They opened studios, filed patents and travelled. Most of them were Western, working in countries that offered an increasing number of businesses selling photography equipment, along with photography clubs and publications.

These pioneers include several scientists who used photography to record their discoveries. The first of them, Anna Atkins, was a botanist who created cyanotype images capturing the outlines of plants. In the 1920s, another scientist, Aenne Biermann, who was keenly interested in mineralogy, began by documenting natural science collections. Berenice Abbott, meanwhile, wanted to illustrate the principles of mechanics and light by means of her abstract compositions and took out several patents.

Many of these women were inventors, like Olive Edis, who created a device for viewing autochromes, or researchers, like Imogen Cunningham, who wrote a thesis on photographic paper and platinum prints. These photographers wrote handbooks and guides and taught in their studios or in schools of photography. Thanks to their role in passing on knowledge, they became figures of authority, imprinting their signature on this booming new profession. Some joined professional associations, like Laure Albin-Guillot in France or Madame Yevonde in Great Britain. As a portraitist of high society who supported the suffragettes, Yevonde promoted the rights of women through her photography. Her American colleague Imogen Cunningham published an article advocating photography as a profession for women as early as 1913.

By setting up their own studios, these women managed to support themselves financially and became independent entrepreneurs who promoted their own names and reputations. A number of them set up studios with evocative names, like Dora Kallmus with the Atelier d'Ora, or the ringl + pit studio run by Ellen Auerbach and Grete Stern, who were innovative figures in the flourishing field of advertising. Working as photographers also offered these women a chance to travel the world, especially if they were photojournalists. One woman, Olive Edis, became one of the first reporters to work in the field, covering the First World War.

Despite these opportunities, a woman photographer's career could be a rocky one. Aware of the difficulties, Wynn Richards chose to work under a male name to give herself greater freedom. Several photographers were scarcely recognized or were forgotten after a period of success, like Zaida Ben-Yúsuf, who came up against financial difficulties, or Jessie Tarbox Beals, who ended her days in poverty. Others faded into the background, like Lucia Moholy, whose photographs were published uncredited. Yet if there is any field where everything is possible, it is that of photography as a form of artistic expression, where women have always pushed back the boundaries. As early as the 1870s, Julia Margaret Cameron was a pioneer of the use of soft focus in her depictions of figures from Arthurian legend. As part of the Pictorialist movement, several women helped to raise photography to the status of an art form, and joined the ranks of the Photo-Secession in New York. Inspired by fine art, they manipulated their prints to heighten the expressiveness of the subjects and composed their images as though they were paintings.

At the turn of the 20th century, several women were among the first to break with Pictorialism and to draw on the specific qualities of the photographic medium in their search for clarity and transparency. They innovated by choosing unusual angles and adopting a direct approach. The west coast of the USA became a creative hub, centred in particular around the figures of Imogen Cunningham and Edward Weston. Weston lived first with Margrethe Mather, then Tina Modotti, followed by Sonya Noskowiak. These women all experimented with the principles promoted by Group f/64, creating geometric compositions, abstract studies and architectural views.

The transition from soft-focus Pictorialism to the quest for modernist transparency was reflected in photographic studios. Portraitists moved away from rigid, fixed, timeless poses and attempted to capture more spontaneous expressions, which gradually helped to shape the image of the active and dynamic 'New Woman'. Conversely, others exaggerated the staged aspects of photography, working in an almost theatrical way and suggesting alternative ways of seeing women. Photography also offered a chance to create subversive self-portraits, as in the case of Gertrud Arndt, who ironically distorted feminine stereotypes, or Marta Astfalck-Vietz, whose images suggest eroticism and gender ambiguity. Olga Spolarich focused on the erotic in her use of photomontage, as did Yva, who created androgynous blurred silhouettes. Questions about gender lay at the heart of the work of Claude Cahun, whose self-portraits blur the distinctions between traditional roles. Eroticism was a feature of the work of photographers who gravitated towards Surrealism, including Dora Maar and Lee Miller. Many of these women manipulated their images through the use of solarization, photograms and multiple exposures.

The inter-war period was marked by a growth in the illustrated press and in avant-garde experimentation. The New Vision photographers would wander the streets of cities, searching for unusual viewpoints. Others observed passers-by with an empathetic eye that foreshadowed the rise of the humanist movement. Several key figures had already turned to documentary work, including Dorothea Lange and Berenice Abbott. Together they helped photographers to rise to the recognized status of artists or creators, thanks to their special powers of observation and ability to tell stories through their images.

The potential for new opportunities also affected the private lives of these women. Some of them were openly lesbian, such as Alice Austen, Claude Cahun and Trude Fleischmann. Others became politically committed, like Tina Modotti. Alice Lex-Nerlinger, a Communist and feminist, created photomontages that criticized the oppression of women. Several women photographers gained professional recognition in areas dominated by men, including the architect Lotte Beese and the designer Marianne Brandt, both of them members of the Bauhaus, or the writer Eudora Welty, whose literary career was crowned by a number of awards. The prize for audacity, however, must surely go to the British-based photographer Edith Tudor-Hart, who was a spy for the Soviet Union.

To the Unknown Photographers

This page is dedicated to all the photographers who are not mentioned in this book, those we could not include, those whose names have been forgotten or whose work has been lost: professional photographers in the fields of portraiture, fashion, photojournalism and advertising; the assistants and editors whose own work was never recognized; those who used photography to document their scientific or sociological research; those who were responsible for capturing the memorable moments of family life and holidays in photo albums, who bought early Kodak cameras or began to take pictures using their mobile phone; those who did not call themselves photographers, and those who did; the teachers, pioneers, amateurs, members of photography clubs, travellers and many others.

Anna Atkins

1799–1871, UK

Anna Atkins's work as a photographer and botanist changed the face of scientific publishing and illustration. In 1823, she began to produce illustrations for Jean-Baptiste de Lamarck's *Genera of Shells*, which was being translated by her father, the naturalist John George Children. She took a keen interest in studying plants and in 1838 became a member of the Botanical Society of London. From 1843 onwards, she pioneered the use of new photographic techniques in her chosen field, making use of the cyanotype process first developed by the astronomer John Herschel, a family friend. This process involves placing an object directly onto light-sensitive paper in order to create a contact image. During development, the outlines of the subject appear on the photogram, which is bright blue in colour.

Atkins used this technique to document British algae and seaweed species, as well as plants and ferns. Her images exhibit university-standard precision and show the potential of photography as a scientific tool. They are also aesthetically striking, forming a herbarium in outline, and are now widely admired as precursors of modern photography.

1. *Pteris aquilina*, cyanotype, 1851.

Pteris aquilina.

Mary Dillwyn
1816–1906, UK

Mary Dillwyn was a pioneering photographer from Wales, whose work has long remained overshadowed by that of her brother, John Dillwyn Llewelyn, another early leader in the field. In the early 1850s, she began to use the calotype process developed by William Henry Fox Talbot, a family friend, and photographed her family, flowers, dolls and pets. Her album illustrates the various pastimes of women from well-to-do circles during the Victorian era, who used this new medium to document their lives and leisure time.

Dillwyn's most striking work is her portraiture, which captures fleeting moments in a style very different from the stiff poses seen in the work of early photography studios. She used a small-format camera with short exposure times that allowed her to capture the natural expressions of her friends and family members. She was one of many amateur photographers who helped to enrich the nascent art of photography.

2. Sally and Mrs Reed, Wales, *c.* 1853.

Sally & Mrs Reed.
Mary Lindsay peeping

Virginia Oldoïni, Countess of Castiglione

1837, Italy–1899, France

Born in Florence, Virginia Oldoïni married Count Francesco Verasis of Castiglione in 1854. A close friend of Victor Emmanuel of Savoy, King of Piedmont, she left for Paris in 1856 to plead the cause of Italian unity with Emperor Napoleon III, eventually becoming his mistress. She returned to Italy the following year, before finally settling in Paris in 1861. After separating from her husband, she frequented aristocratic and political circles before leading a more discreet life, shrouded in mystery, after the fall of the Empire in 1870. Although he never met her, the poet Robert de Montesquiou was obsessed by her and collected objects she had once owned, publishing a biography of her entitled *La Divine Comtesse* (1913).

Between 1856 and 1895, the Countess of Castiglione was responsible for more than four hundred self-portraits, taken in collaboration with Pierre-Louis Pierson, a photographer for the imperial court. She appears in them wearing a variety of costumes, with props and settings that she chose herself, representing fictional characters such as the Queen of Hearts, or the heroines of contemporary theatre and opera. The photographs taken under her direction were then printed in the form of calling cards or enlarged and painted. These multiple versions of the same portrait, which were distributed during her lifetime, are very rare. Famed for her beauty, the countess would sometimes pose with a mirror, to highlight the artifice of the scene, and even appeared with bare legs, in the guise of a prostitute. Over the years, she also recorded the passage of time as it changed her body. An early practitioner of performance art and fictionalized autobiography, she used her work to build a mythical aura, associating herself with the intrigues and sophisticated life of the imperial court as well as with audacity and scandal.

3. *Scherzo di Follia*, portrait of the Countess of Castiglione taken by Pierre-Louis Pierson, 1860s.

Lady Clementina Hawarden

1822–65, UK

Lady Clementina Hawarden is known for her portraits of her
daughters, which are both sophisticated and theatrical. She began
her experiments in photography with stereoscopic images of
landscapes: two shots of the same subject taken from positions an
eye's width apart, which created a three-dimensional effect when
viewed together. She then used the same technique for her portraits,
before opting for larger-format stand-alone images. Her daughters
were to become her favourite models. She had them pose indoors
and outdoors, using natural light to emphasize the shadows and
drapery, dressing them in elegant costumes and posing them in
front of architectural forms and elaborate backdrops. She used
fabrics and mirrors to create these carefully crafted compositions,
focusing on expressions that were sometimes provocative and
sometimes romantic.

The Photographic Society of London exhibited her 'Photographic
Studies' and 'Studies from Life' in 1863 and 1864, awarding her two
silver medals. She died of pneumonia at the age of forty-two. Her
work, archived at the Victoria & Albert Museum in London, has
gained new recognition since the 1970s for its formal qualities and
the way it validated photography as a form of artistic expression.

4. Study from Life (Isabella Grace and Clementina Maude), c. 1863–64.

D605

Julia Margaret Cameron
1815, India–1879, Ceylon (Sri Lanka)

Julia Margaret Cameron studied in France and Britain before marrying in 1838 and having six children. The family settled in the Isle of Wight in 1860. Cameron was given her first camera in around 1863 and soon began asking her friends and family to pose for her. Inspired by classical culture, she photographed scenes of madonnas, angels and allegorical motifs. Her figures were usually either religious or literary, and she created costumes and sets that suggest a medieval atmosphere, reminiscent of Pre-Raphaelite paintings. She experimented with close-ups and made unusual use of soft focus, creating a kind of halo around her models.

She also produced portraits of her friends, including the astronomer Sir John Herschel and the poet Lord Alfred Tennyson. In the 1870s, she illustrated a collection of Tennyson's works, retelling the legend of King Arthur in compositions with clever lighting that featured figures such as Guinevere, Lancelot and Merlin, portrayed by her friends and family.

She sold her prints to the Victoria & Albert Museum and took part in exhibitions, which gave rise to some criticism that the soft focus of her images was due to a lack of technical expertise. Nevertheless, it was this innovative approach to the medium, a hallmark of her work, that eventually helped her gain recognition as a pioneer of 19th-century art photography. She was admired by the avant-garde Pictorialists, in particular Alfred Stieglitz, who regarded her as a key figure.

5. Sir John Herschel, astronomer, 1867.

Frances Benjamin Johnston

1864–1952, USA

Frances Benjamin Johnston enrolled in art courses in Paris and Washington DC, where she trained in photography in the late 1880s. She became known for her portraits of politicians and produced images and texts for illustrated magazines. Encouraged by her success, she published articles highlighting photography by women and encouraged other women to enter the profession, explaining how they should proceed in order to make money out of photography. She took part in the 1900 Universal Exhibition in Paris, where she curated an exhibition of photography by women and gave an accompanying lecture.

An important figure in the Pictorialist movement, she joined the Photo-Secession founded by Alfred Stieglitz. She was also interested in progressive education and documented the activities of several schools in the USA. During the 1910s, she photographed architectural scenes and landscapes, especially gardens, experimenting with colour. From the late 1920s, she headed a major campaign to document the historical heritage of the American South and published several books on the subject. Her archives, now at the Library of Congress, are testament to her role as an important pioneer of American photography at the turn of the century.

6. Self-portrait, *c.* 1890.

Eveleen Myers

1856–1937, UK

Eveleen Myers appeared on the British artistic scene at the turn of the century. She frequented the Pre-Raphaelite painters, two of whom, John Everett Millais and George Frederic Watts, painted her portrait. In 1880, she married the poet and classicist Frederic Myers. She took her first photographs in 1888, using her children as models and taking inspiration from Pre-Raphaelite compositions and from Julia Margaret Cameron, of whose work she owned some prints. She also photographed eminent figures in Victorian society, using a more direct style and showing them in natural light.

Her husband was involved in research in the fields of psychology and paranormal phenomena and would regularly invite mediums into the family circle. Eveleen Myers's portrait of Leonora Piper, a famous American clairvoyant, gives her profile a kind of soft halo, evoking her talents. On the death of her husband in 1901, Myers gave up photography and dedicated herself to publishing his writings.

7. Leonora Piper, medium, 1890.

Alice Austen
1866–1952, USA

Alice Austen, who grew up in a prosperous family in Staten Island, New York, was fascinated by photography from the age of ten. She became a seasoned amateur photographer and took self-portraits and pictures of members of her family. She also documented the environment, local beaches and lakes, and the activities of the tennis club of which she was an active member. She illustrated a book by her friend Violet Ward, *Bicycling for Ladies*, published in 1896. She travelled in the USA and in Europe, taking her bulky equipment with her, and in 1899 she met Gertrude Tate, with whom she was to spend the rest of her life. In 1914, she founded a gardening club and carefully tended the grounds surrounding her family home.

The wealth she had inherited dwindled during the 1920s and disappeared with the Wall Street crash in 1929. Austen and Tate then opened a tea room, but it did not make enough money to support them and Austen had to sell the family home. She was living in a poorhouse in 1950 when her work was rediscovered thanks to the publication of a book on the history of American women; this provided her with enough funds to move into a nursing home. Her photographs of street traders in New York and of leisure activities, social life and the landscapes of Staten Island were later put on display in a museum dedicated to her work, established in the house where she had lived. She is recognized as a major figure in LGBT history, breaking with convention to live with her partner, and creating a number of images that subvert gender roles, having no hesitation about photographing herself in male dress. In 1891, she posed with her childhood friends, forming two embracing couples, and entitled the image 'The Darned Club', from a nickname they had been given as children.

8. 'The Darned Club', Staten Island, New York, 29 October 1891.

"The
Darned
Club"
.A.A

Hannah Maynard

1834, UK–1918, Canada

Hannah Maynard emigrated to Canada with her husband Richard in 1852, where he opened a shoe shop in Bowmanville, Ontario. They settled in Victoria in 1862, where Hannah set up a professional photography studio. She specialized in portraits, while her husband photographed landscapes that documented various regions of the country. Her portraits were presented in the form of calling cards or larger-format prints, with elaborate lighting effects and background scenery.

In the 1880s, she began to experiment with photomontage and image manipulation. Her greeting cards, in the form of portraits of babies and children photographed in her studio over the previous year, met with great success. These photomontages were then inserted into larger compositions, featuring geometric motifs and sometimes including hundreds of faces. In some of her portraits, the model's head seems to be posed on a pedestal, like a statue. She also took self-portraits, using multiple exposures to make herself appear several times in the same image, creating a dreamlike or humorous effect.

9. Self-portrait, tea time, 1893.

Belle Johnson

1864–1945, USA

Belle Johnson became manager of a photographic studio in Monroe City, Missouri, in 1890, after working there as an apprentice for several weeks. Throughout her life, she took portraits of the people of the region, gaining a local, then national, reputation thanks to competitions and exhibitions. An entrepreneur and active member of various professional associations, she never stopped learning new techniques and improving her portrait art, creating carefully orchestrated photographs. She also produced compositions with children, still lifes of flowers, and portraits of dogs and cats, distributing her work in the form of postcards.

Always in search of unusual subjects, she produced an enigmatic photograph that broke with the usual form of studio portrait: three women shown from the back, their undone hair tumbling to the ground to form the focus of the image, which is both provocative and intriguing.

10. Three women with long hair, *c*. 1895.

Zaida Ben-Yúsuf

1869, UK–1933, USA

Zaida Ben-Yúsuf was born in London to an Algerian father and German mother. She moved to the USA in the mid-1890s to work as a milliner, following in the footsteps of her mother who had emigrated a few years earlier. In 1897, she opened a portrait studio which became very popular. Her photographs of actors, artists, explorers and politicians were widely published in the press. She exhibited her work in Europe and the USA and took fashion photographs for illustrated magazines.

At the same time, she published travel journals and wrote pieces on fashion and photography. In 1903, she travelled to Japan, after which she moved between Paris, London and New York, before applying for US citizenship in 1914. Faced with financial difficulties, she turned to design and fashion again in the 1920s.

Through her international career, ranging from fashion to portraiture via artistic photography and writing, she became a pioneer who earned a lasting reputation both in galleries and in leading magazines.

11. The Odour of Pomegranates, 1899.

Gertrude Käsebier

1852–1934, USA

Gertrude Stanton grew up in Brooklyn and married a businessman of German origin, Eduard Käsebier, in 1874. She devoted herself to her family before studying art in the 1880s and then specializing in photography. She opened a studio in 1897 and showed her work in exhibitions. In 1902, she became a founder member of the Photo-Secession, along with Edward Steichen, Alfred Stieglitz and Clarence H. White, who all believed that photography should be recognized as an art form. In 1910, she founded and chaired the Women's Professional Photographers' Association of America. She broke with Stieglitz in 1916, when he moved away from Pictorialism. Käsebier became involved in setting up a new movement, Pictorial Photographers of America, which published the magazine *Platinum Print*.

An adherent of Pictorialism, Käsebier is known for her portraits and images of motherhood. Influenced by her training as a painter, she sought expressiveness and a sense of intimacy, and often manipulated her prints to obtain the effect she wanted. Her work has been shown in a number of retrospectives since the 1970s and one of her images was featured on a US postage stamp in 2002.

12. Evelyn Nesbit, 1903.

Jessie Tarbox Beals

1870, Canada–1942, USA

Jessie Tarbox Beals began her career as a teacher in Williamsburg, Massachusetts, and then started to take photographs in 1888, offering local students four portraits for the price of one US dollar. On her marriage in 1897, she gave up teaching and from 1900 onwards devoted herself to photography. Together with her husband, she set up a service taking portraits in people's homes. She then moved to Buffalo, New York, and worked for local newspapers, becoming one of the first women photojournalists. She had an enterprising personality and managed to establish herself as a key photographer at the Louisiana Purchase Exposition in 1904, working for a number of newspapers. She was innovative in that she took photographs in series rather than in isolation, devised photojournalism projects before the accompanying articles had been written, and took photographs that were more than mere illustrations.

When she moved to New York, she was commissioned to take portraits of figures from the art world. She left her husband in 1917 and settled in Greenwich Village, at the heart of the burgeoning artistic community, where she opened a tea shop and gallery. Like many other women photographers, she remained freelance rather than working full-time for any one publication. She documented artistic life in Greenwich and the experiments in progressive education being carried out there. In 1928, she travelled to California to photograph the estates of movie moguls. She died in poverty in New York, and her work and pioneering role were mostly forgotten until her rediscovery in the late 1970s.

13. Blizzard in Times Square, New York, *c.* 1905.

Alice Boughton
1865–1943, USA

After training in Paris and New York, Alice Boughton worked as an assistant in Gertrude Käsebier's studio. She opened her own studio in New York in 1890, photographing figures from the literary and theatrical scene. In 1928, she published a collection of her portraits, *Photographing the Famous*.

Renowned as a professional photographer, she was also known for her landscapes, studies of children, and female nudes. She staged her subjects meticulously, placing them in natural or allegorical settings and emphasizing the elegant postures of the models through the use of elaborate lighting. A member of the Photo-Secession, she exhibited with that group, sharing their love of soft-focus images and their belief that photography should be raised to the status of an art form. Her allegorical image 'Dawn', showing a female nude seen from the back, facing the rising sun from a river bank, with a transparent sphere in her hands, was published in *Camera Work* in 1909. Her prints can now be found in the collections of several museums and justify her ranking as one of the first avant-garde photographers.

14. Two women under a tree, 1906.

Anne Brigman

1869, Hawaii–1950, USA

Born in Hawaii, Anne Brigman moved to California and trained as a painter before turning to photography in 1902. Her photographs were published in *Camera Work*, the magazine run by Alfred Stieglitz, founder of the Photo-Secession, and she became a member of the avant-garde group. She photographed allegorical female nudes in natural landscapes, allowing the sinuous forms of the trees to echo the dramatic poses of the models. Her images symbolize a union between feminine strength and the Californian landscape.

She also photographed the effects of the erosion of sand by wind and sea, in a manner close to abstraction. In 1949, she published a collection of her photographs and poems, *Songs of a Pagan*. A prominent figure in West Coast artistic circles, she came to international fame by taking part in competitions and exhibitions.

15. The Cleft in the Rock, 1912.

Minya Diez-Dührkoop

1873–1929, Germany

At the age of fourteen, Minya Diez-Dührkoop began working in her father's studio in Hamburg. The business produced portraits as well as architectural photographs and reproductions of art works. They enjoyed great success and branches were opened in Berlin, leaving Minya in sole charge of the Hamburg studio. The Dührkoop family's work became increasingly well-known and was included in a number of exhibitions, especially during their trips to the UK and the USA. Through their travels, they had the opportunity to meet foreign photographers and become part of avant-garde artistic circles.

Influenced by Pictorialism, Minya Diez-Dührkoop saw photography as an independent art form. She was particularly interested in contemporary dance photography and went on to develop an intimate and sophisticated form of portrait art. In these works, she highlighted the grace and elegance of her models, mostly women, by showing them in close up and in natural poses, far removed from the rigidity of photographic convention.

16. Clotilde von Derp-Sakharoff, German dancer, 1912.

Clotilde von Derp

Adelaide Hanscom

1876–1932, USA

After studying painting, in 1902 Adelaide Hanscom opened a photography studio in San Francisco with Blanche Cummings. She became renowned for her studies, landscapes and portraits, after showing her work in a number of exhibitions. She created illustrations for an English translation of the *Rubáiyát of Omar Khayyám*, a 12th-century collection of Persian poetry, using major figures from the Californian literary world as models. She regularly retouched her allegorical images, shot in a Pictorialist style, and drew additional details directly onto the glass plate. The book enjoyed great success, but the negatives were destroyed in the San Francisco earthquake and fire of 1906.

Hanscom moved to Seattle, where she opened a new studio. She illustrated Elizabeth Barrett Browning's poems, *Sonnets from the Portuguese*, placing her images inside decorative frames. This series featured children and women wearing long draped garments, posed in painted or natural settings. She also photographed her own children to illustrate a book of nursery rhymes and poems for children. Her sophisticated compositions are an early example of the potential of photography as illustration.

17. Sonnets from the Portuguese, 1916.

Olive Edis
1876–1955, UK

Olive Edis opened her first studio in Norfolk in 1905, together with her sister Katherine. She went on to set up several studios in London and outside it. She photographed members of the royal family, suffragettes, and fishermen and their families. Her work is marked by a direct approach, using natural light, which lends spontaneity and authenticity to her subjects. She was a pioneer in her use of colour, experimenting with the autochrome process from 1912 onwards, and she even patented a device for viewing her images.

In 1918, the National War Museum in London (later the Imperial War Museum) commissioned her to document the work of the British women's military services and to photograph the battlefields of the Great War in France and Flanders, which meant that she became one of the first female war reporters. Her 1918 self-portrait, with her bulky equipment and a cap adorned with the museum's initials, bears witness to her pioneering role and the uncompromising style for which she became famous.

18. Self-portrait in a cap with the badge of the National War Museum, 1918.

Claude Cahun
1894, France–1954, Jersey

Lucy Schwob, who studied philosophy and literature at the Sorbonne, adopted the pseudonym Claude Cahun in 1917. An associate of the Surrealists, Cahun worked in the theatre and used photography to question gender norms, using costumes, masks and techniques of doubling and reflection. Their self-portraits sometimes show them dressed as a man, sometimes as a woman, and sometimes as an androgynous figure, with long hair or a shaven head.

In 1930, they published *Aveux non avenus*, a series of texts and photomontages created jointly with partner Suzanne Malherbe, who used the name Marcel Moore. In 1934, Cahun wrote a pamphlet entitled *Les paris sont ouverts* that emphasized the subversive power of art in the face of the rise of totalitarianism. Their poetic and political beliefs were expressed in the 'Puppet' series, based around a figure made out of newspaper, and the 'Theatre' series, which features a wooden artist's mannequin under a glass dome. At the 1936 Surrealist Exhibition, Cahun exhibited 'object assemblages' made from twigs, utensils, bones, feathers and fabric. These were used the following year to illustrate a collection of poems by Lise Deharme entitled *Le Cœur de pic*.

When Cahun settled in Jersey in 1937, they turned to political action against the occupying troops. They were arrested by the Gestapo and liberated on 8 May 1945. Cahun's work, rediscovered in the early 1980s, is a fascinating example of the pioneering subversion of gender codes and identities.

19. Self-portrait (with shaved head), 1920.

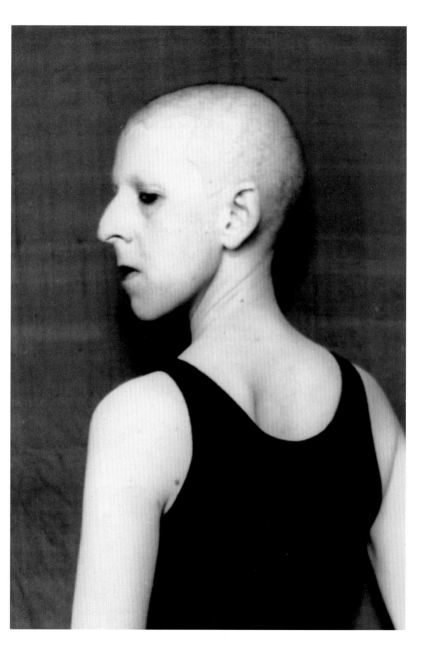

Charlotte Rudolph
1896–1983, Germany

Charlotte Rudolph opened a photography studio in Dresden in the 1920s. She specialized in portraiture and dance photography. Her images highlight the graceful poses of dancers via the clever use of shadows projected onto plain backdrops. She worked with renowned choreographers, including Gret Palucca and Chinita Ullman, who ran dance schools, the opera director Margarete Wallmann, and Mary Wigman, a pioneer of Expressionist dance and dance therapy.

She paid tribute to Wigman in a composition that combined multiple images of her hands making elaborate gestures, shown in isolation against a neutral ground. This avant-garde image reflects Rudolph's photographic and choreographic experimentation. Her collaborations with Gret Palucca also had an influence on the innovations of the Bauhaus, where different realms of creativity were allowed to intersect. Rudolph's archives and her studio were destroyed during the Second World War.

20. Hands of the dancer and choreographer Mary Wigman, 1920.

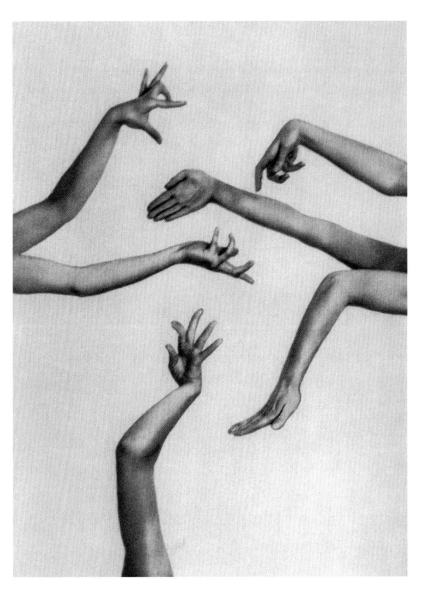

Margrethe Mather

1885–1952, USA

Born into a Mormon family in Salt Lake City, Margrethe Mather moved to San Francisco in 1906, where she frequented artistic circles. In 1912, she relocated to Los Angeles, where she met the photographer Edward Weston through the Los Angeles Camera Club. The two worked as a creative couple for some ten years and she took several portraits of him, which reflect their joint experiments. In the 1920s, she entered into another creative partnership, this time with the artist Billy Justema.

She was an innovative portraitist and her work is notable for the dramatic use of soft focus and repeating shadows, which seem to create a double of the subject portrayed. Sometimes her figures are shown in close-up, in profile and with a pensive gaze; on other occasions, they are positioned within a larger geometric frame. She subsequently turned to a more direct approach, often including decorative elements such as drapery. Although Weston's name is better remembered than that of Mather, she was nonetheless an influential artist on the West Coast scene.

21. Edward Weston, 1921.

Dora Kallmus
(Madame d'Ora)
1881–1963, Austria

Dora Kallmus grew up in Vienna and in 1905 she became the first
female member of the Association of Austrian Photographers. She
found great success among the Viennese elite when she opened
a studio, for which she chose a name that sounded elegant and
French, the 'Atelier d'Ora'. Her camera captured actors, musicians,
artists and even the Hungarian imperial family. She was much
sought after for her spontaneous and natural style, a far cry from
the rigid poses typical of contemporary portraits. In 1925, she set up
a studio in Paris, where she photographed eminent figures from the
world of fashion, including the designer Coco Chanel, and worked
for fashion magazines.

Although she converted to Catholicism in 1919, her origins
were Jewish and she was obliged to go into hiding during the
Second World War. After the war, she turned to new subjects,
taking photographs of refugee camps in Austria and the
slaughterhouses of Paris.

Her work provides a detailed record of the art scene between
the wars and serves as a chronicle of the glamorous world of
Paris fashion.

22. Anita Berber, German dancer, 1922.

Tina Modotti

1896, Italy–1942, Mexico

Born into a working-class family in Italy, Tina Modotti emigrated to the USA in 1913. She worked as a seamstress before experimenting with acting in San Francisco's Italian community in 1917. After moving to Los Angeles, she became an actress and a model for the photographer Edward Weston, later becoming his mistress. Together they left for Mexico, where she ran his photographic studio. From 1924 onwards, she documented the socialist art of the Mexican muralist movement, who depicted Mexican workers and culture. Her political commitment took precedence over the formal approach preferred by Edward Weston and she stayed on in Mexico when he returned to the USA.

She joined the Mexican Communist Party in 1927 and photographed her adopted country, focusing mainly on women, folklore and religious art. She was forced to leave Mexico in 1930 after being suspected of involvement in a political assassination plot. She moved on to Moscow and then to Paris. During the Spanish Civil War, she worked for the Spanish section of International Red Aid. She returned to Mexico under a false name two years before her death.

Tina Modotti's work is marked by her political beliefs and bears witness to Mexican traditions and the living conditions of the poorer classes. Her prints, with their subtle tints ranging through every shade of grey, echo the experiments of modernism by isolating parts of the body or capturing urban and architectural details.

23. Open Doors, Mexico City, 1925.

Lucia Moholy

1894, Czech Republic–1989, Switzerland

After studying art history, philosophy and philology in Prague, Lucia Schulz worked for German publishing houses. She married the artist László Moholy-Nagy in 1921 and they settled in Weimar, where he taught at the Bauhaus, the art school that was the epicentre of modernist experimentation in the fields of design and architecture. She became her husband's colleague at that institution and together they produced photograms, although these were often attributed to him alone. After the Bauhaus moved to Dessau, she photographed its new buildings and took portraits of some of the major figures who were involved in it, opting mainly for close-ups that captured facial expressions in detail. These included the founder of the Bauhaus, Walter Gropius, and Edith Tschichold, wife of the graphic artist Jan Tschichold. Her direct, frontal approach was inspired by the principles of the New Objectivity movement.

After she and László Moholy-Nagy separated in 1929, Lucia Moholy began to teach photography in Berlin. She fled to Paris and then to London in 1933, following the arrest of her partner, the Communist deputy Theodor Neubauer. She had to leave her photographic archives behind and they were subsequently published without being credited to her. In 1939, she published a historical survey entitled *A Hundred Years of Photography*. After the war, she took on documentary assignments in the Middle East for UNESCO. In 1972, she published a book on the Bauhaus, aiming to reclaim her rightful place in a movement dominated by men.

24. László Moholy-Nagy, 1925–26.

Trude Fleischmann

1895, Austria–1990, USA

Trude Fleischmann, who came from a well-to-do Jewish family, was fascinated by photography from childhood onwards. An admirer of Madame d'Ora's portrait photography, she became an apprentice in her Vienna studio, but only stayed there for two weeks as her mentor considered her too slow. She went on to work with Hermann Schieberth and then opened her own studio in 1920 with financial help from her family. She took portraits of local artistic personalities and her studio became a cultural hub. Her portraits were published in illustrated magazines, but some of her images of dancers caused a scandal because they were considered shockingly erotic.

She never married but had several relationships with women, including her student Helen Post, who helped her settle in New York when she was forced to leave Austria after the Anschluss in 1938. She opened a new studio with Frank Elmer, another Viennese émigré, and took photographs of the expatriate community while also working for *Vogue* magazine. Like her female contemporaries, Fleischmann found photography a gratifying pursuit at a time when this flourishing profession offered new opportunities to daring women.

25. Wilhelm Furtwängler, conductor, *c.* 1926.

Germaine Krull

1897, Poland–1985, Germany

Germaine Krull studied photography in Munich before taking part in the 1919 Spartacist uprising. She moved to Paris in 1926, where she worked as a fashion photographer. In 1928, she published the portfolio *Metal*, a series of images of metal architecture, bridges and cranes from innovative angles, making a major contribution to the New Vision movement. She also took on photojournalism assignments for *VU* magazine, documenting working-class districts of Paris with her portable Icarette camera. Her photographs of the urban landscapes and night-time lights of the capital were collected in the book *100 × Paris* (1929). A prolific creator of photobooks, the following year she published a portfolio of nudes, offering deconstructed views of the female body, and in 1931 she illustrated a novel by Georges Simenon, *The Madwoman of Itteville*, inventing the photo-novel genre. She was a car enthusiast and published books tracing her road trips, including *La Route Paris-Biarritz* (1930) and *La Route de Paris à la Méditerranée* (1931).

Her varied career and avant-garde work are characterized by an interest in photographing gestures and hands, unusual perspectives, and a passion for travel. She went to Brazil in 1940 to work for the Free French and in 1942 was sent to Brazzaville where she ran a photographic propaganda service. In 1943, she went to Algiers, then stopped off in the south of France, travelled on to Alsace and recorded the liberation of the Vaihingen an der Enz concentration camp in Germany. In 1946, she settled in Bangkok, where she managed the Oriental Hotel until 1966. A follower of Buddhism, she documented the religious heritage of Thailand and Burma and devoted herself to the cause of Tibetans in exile.

26. Publicity shot for Paul Poiret, 1926.

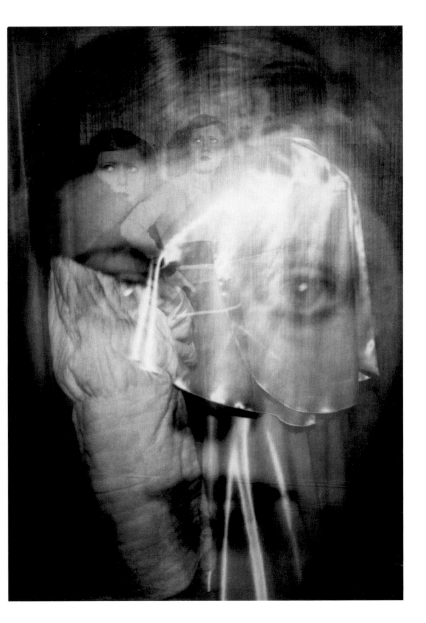

Lotte Beese
1903, Germany–1988, Netherlands

After training as a shorthand typist, Lotte Beese settled in Dresden where she enrolled in weaving classes and met students from the Bauhaus. She decided to join the Bauhaus herself, and studied from 1926 to 1928 with artists such as Josef Albers and Wassily Kandinsky, before specializing in textile design and then in architecture. After qualifying as an architect, she worked in Czechoslovakia, the Soviet Union and the Netherlands. She worked on the post-war rebuilding of Rotterdam, designing plans for a number of city districts in a functionalist style.

An active photographer during her time at the Bauhaus, she took portraits of members of the school and images of student life. Her avant-garde compositions, playing with reflections, shadows and close-ups, are now in the collections of several international museums. A contributor to the visual experiments of the Bauhaus, she became an established architect at a time when this was still a profession traditionally reserved for men.

27. Self-portrait, 1927.

Marta Astfalck-Vietz

1901–94, Germany

Marta Astfalck-Vietz opened her first studio in Berlin in 1927, specializing in nudes, portraits, dance images, still lifes and advertising. Active until 1936, she was inspired by avant-garde films and choreography to create subversive photographs and self-portraits, imbued with black humour and eroticism. The staged scenes were based on photo-manipulations and montages made up of multiple negatives.

She questioned gender and racial identities at a time when these topics were highly controversial. Whether depicting herself masked or costumed, in the guise of a goddess or a high-society lady, she would evoke a dreamlike atmosphere and a sense of melancholy. She even staged a kind of photographic suicide, somewhere between a macabre joke and a Surrealist vision, in which her apparently severed head appears to be preserved in a bell-jar, contrasting with the sinuous nudes visible in the painting in the background.

She then gave up photography and took up interior design, painted watercolours of flowers and began teaching. Nearly all of her negatives disappeared during the bombing of Berlin in 1943. Her work, rediscovered in 1989, is now archived at the Berlinische Galerie. Her strange and witty photographs make a radical contribution to the history of women's self-portraiture.

28. Suicide in Spirit, 1927.

Rogi André
(Rosa Klein)
1905, Hungary–1970, France

After studying art in Budapest, Rosa Klein moved to Paris in
1925. Four years later, she married one of her compatriots, the
photographer André Kertész; they separated in 1932. She became
known as a portrait photographer under the pseudonym Rogi André,
choosing unusually to visit her models rather than working in her
own studio. Her carefully composed images integrate figures into the
geometry of their environment. Lighting is often focused on the face
to bring out the gaze of the subject, who is often depicted frontally.

Rogi André is best known for her portraits of major figures
from the art world, including Fernand Léger, Dora Maar and André
Breton. One of her images, published in 1937 in André Breton's
book L'Amour fou, captures an underwater performance by the
dancer Jacqueline Lamba, her nude body undulating in the water,
which distorts her shape. It is an example of André's photographic
experimentation and reflects her affinity with the avant-garde.
This image had already been published in the Surrealist review
Minotaure two years previously. After exhibiting in Paris, New
York and Copenhagen, André devoted herself to painting from
the 1950s onwards.

29. Nude, 1927.

Aenne Biermann

1898–1933, Germany

Born into a prosperous family in North Rhine-Westphalia, Aenne Biermann began photographing her own children in 1921. A keen mineralogist, she met the geologist Rudolf Hundt in 1926 and he gave her her first commission: making a photographic record of his collection of specimens. Her scientific work led her to experiment with close-up studies of plants and with portrait photography. Her quest for realism made her a central figure in the German New Objectivity movement. She would sometimes allow the frame of the image to crop off the edges of a face, as a means of highlighting the sitter's gaze. Her photograph of a tree shows only a single branch with angular forms that draw the eye towards the detail of the twigs and buds. She photographed still lifes in a simplified style that revealed the geometry of everyday objects, and also experimented with photomontage and double exposures, as in the photograph combining an inverted view of the Champs-Élysées in Paris with the face of a woman.

Her reputation grew after her work was featured in exhibitions and major publications. A monograph featuring sixty of her photographs was published in 1930. Her work fell into obscurity after her early death at the age of thirty-five in 1933 and many of her negatives were destroyed under the Nazi regime.

30. Champs-Élysées, Paris, *c.* 1928.

Florence Henri

1893, USA–1982, France

Born in New York to an American mother and a French father, Florence Henri grew up in Europe. She moved to Berlin at the age of nineteen, where she frequented artistic circles and met several avant-garde figures, including John Heartfield and László Moholy-Nagy. In 1924, she moved to Paris where she studied painting, first at the Académie Montparnasse then at the Académie Moderne, before enrolling in the foundation course at the Bauhaus in Dessau in summer 1927.

Inspired by Constructivism and Cubism, her work explores space by using fragmentation and multiple perspectives, often with the aid of mirrors. Known for her portraits and self-portraits, she experimented with nudes, advertising images and still lifes, as well as creating 'abstract' compositions by using double exposures or photomontages of multiple negatives. She also taught photography to students who included Gisèle Freund and Lisette Model. In 1929, she opened her own professional studio. In the same year, her images were shown in Stuttgart at the 'Film und Foto' exhibition, followed by shows in New York, Paris and London. After being somewhat forgotten for a time, her work was rediscovered in the mid-1970s.

31. Self-portrait, 1928.

Imogen Cunningham

1883–1976, USA

Imogen Cunningham started painting and drawing when she was still a child. At the age of eighteen, she bought her first camera and began to teach herself photography. She studied chemistry at the University of Washington and then worked in Seattle in the studio of the photographer Edward Curtis, renowned for his portraits of Native Americans. In 1909, she was awarded a grant by her university's women's association, which enabled her to continue her chemistry studies in Dresden in Germany and to write a thesis entitled 'Modern Processes of Photography', in which she discussed photographic paper and platinum printing.

She returned to the USA via Paris and London. In New York, she met photographer and gallery owner Alfred Stieglitz and he introduced her to Gertrude Käsebier, who ran a photography studio. Cunningham then opened her own portrait studio in Seattle, specializing in photographs in the Pictorialist style. On her marriage in 1915, she closed her studio. She had three sons and often photographed her family and the plants in her garden, concentrating on details and isolating abstract forms with great precision. In 1932, she and the photographer Edward Weston founded Group f/64, which moved away from the Pictorialist style in search of greater precision and clarity.

Cunningham also experimented with multiple exposures and took portraits of famous figures, including the dancer Martha Graham. After her divorce in 1934, she worked for magazines including *Vanity Fair* and *Life*. Her work was exhibited at the Museum of Modern Art and at Limelight, a photography gallery in New York founded by Helen Gee. Cunningham wrote a number of texts on photography, including a plea to give women greater access to the profession, which was published in 1913.

32. Banana plant, before 1929.

Laure Albin Guillot

1879–1962, France

Laure Albin Guillot became known in the first half of the 1920s for her fashion photography and very elaborate portraits. Her classical style was based on a pared-back approach to light and soft focus. She also photographed nudes inspired by statues. In 1931, she published *Micrographie décorative*, a collection of microscopic images of minerals and plants that are fascinating in their ornamental geometry.

The same elegant and pared-back approach dominated her commercial work, in which she photographed luxury products, cosmetics and pharmaceuticals. In 1933, she published *Photographie publicitaire*, a work on the theory of advertising photography, which established her reputation. In addition, she published limited-edition artist's books, which combined images and texts, produced in conjunction with writers such as Paul Valéry.

An influential institutional figure, she was director of the photographic archives of the Direction Générale des Beaux-Arts and of the Cinémathèque Nationale, and chaired the Union Féminine des Carrières Libérales et Commerciales, an organization that promoted the interests of professional women. She advocated the recognition of photography as an art and a craft, based on strict technical expertise and a demanding aesthetic approach.

33. Micrograph, *c.* 1929.

Eva Besnyö
1910, Hungary–2003, Netherlands

After an apprenticeship in the studio of portraitist and advertising photographer József Pécsi in Budapest, Eva Besnyö moved to Berlin in 1930. Inspired by the experimental work of the New Objectivity and New Vision movements, she used her Rolleiflex 6 × 6 to shoot from innovative angles, playing with reflections and the effects of high-angle shots and fragmentation. A committed left-winger, she documented working-class areas and workers. She left for the Netherlands two years later and opened a studio in Amsterdam, where she became close to the New Construction architects and photographed their work. She also curated the first international photography exhibition at the Stedelijk Museum, entitled 'Foto '37'.

As she was of Jewish origin, she was forced to live in secret during the war and only emerged in public again in 1944 after concocting a fictional genealogy. She photographed the ruins of the old town of Rotterdam after it was destroyed by air raids. In the late 1950s, she began to work in photojournalism, including a series on women doing men's jobs. During the 1970s, she recorded the activities of the Dolle Mina, the Dutch women's movement, of which she was an active member. This commitment reflects the political commitment that marked her career as a liberated woman. One of her early photographs features a scene enacted by shadows, with the photographer's fingers almost touching those of her sister, perhaps as a female reenactment of the outstretched hands in Michelangelo's *The Creation of Adam*.

34. Eva and Magda, Hungary, 1929.

Marianne Breslauer

1909, Germany–2001, Switzerland

Born into a Jewish family in Berlin, Marianne Breslauer trained as a photographer between 1927 and 1929. She met and portrayed figures from the artistic circles of Berlin, including the photographer Umbo. In 1929, she left for Paris, where she took street photographs inspired by the work of André Kertész, whom she admired. She concentrated on details, like the hats of two men seen from the back, and chose unusual perspectives, such as her high-angle shot of the café La Rotonde. On her return to Berlin the following year, she worked for the Ullstein publishing house and took portraits of artists. She continued this work in Paris in 1932, photographing Pablo Picasso and Ambroise Vollard. Her images were published in illustrated magazines. In 1933, she travelled around Spain with the Swiss writer Annemarie Schwarzenbach, but few of the images were published in Germany because of her Jewish origins.

The rise of Nazism put a brake on her career. She left for the Netherlands and married the art dealer Walter Feilchenfeldt. At the beginning of the Second World War, the couple moved to Zurich where they set up an art gallery.

35. La Rotonde, Paris, 1930.

Alice Lex-Nerlinger

1893–1975, Germany

After studying painting and graphic art, Alice Lex-Nerlinger was inspired by the avant-garde artistic experiments happening in Berlin in the 1920s and began creating photograms and political photomontages. She focused on simple graphic compositions, casting a critical eye on issues such as labour, machines, war, capitalism, class differences and censorship. A committed feminist, she critiqued the ban on abortions and the living conditions of women. From her earliest photomontages, which she created to illustrate a children's book dedicated to her son, she retained the same love of clarity and education, promoting a visual and radical dialectic based on schematic forms, repeat motifs and diagonals.

Together with her husband, the artist Oskar Nerlinger, she joined the Communist Party and designed posters. She could not continue her art under the Nazi regime and destroyed hundreds of her works in fear of her house being searched. After the Second World War, she worked mainly as a portrait photographer and graphic artist.

36. The Aeroplane, 1929.

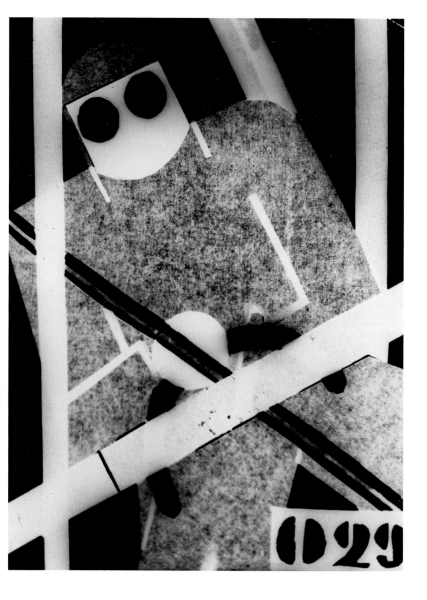

Madame Yevonde

1893–1975, UK

From the age of sixteen, Yevonde Cumbers Middleton supported the cause of the English suffragettes and their demand for the right to vote. Wanting to adopt a profession that would protect her independence, she decided to become a photographer. She trained under the high-society portraitist Lallie Charles and opened her own studio under the name Madame Yevonde in 1914. She enjoyed great success with her innovative portraits that made use of sophisticated poses and sets. She also created fashion and advertising photographs that were published in the illustrated press. In 1921, she exhibited her work at the Royal Photographic Society and became a member of the Professional Photographers' Association, where she gave a lecture in which she stressed the contribution of women to the genre of portrait photography.

In the 1930s, she turned to colour photography, using the new Vivex colour process, which allowed her to capture the sheen of skin and the bold colours of clothes. In 1935, she shot a series of portraits of fashionable women dressed as goddesses and mythological figures. She travelled to New York in 1936 and a number of her images were exhibited at the Museum of Modern Art the following year. Today her work is recognized for its originality and innovative use of colour and vivid hues.

37. Alison Hore-Ruthven and her husband John Barran,
The Sketch magazine, 1929.

HALF A TWIN AND HER BETTER HALF.

FORMERLY THE HON. ALISON HORE-RUTHVEN: THE HON. MRS. JOHN BARRAN WITH MR. JOHN BARRAN.

This amusing composite portrait shows the married " Ruthven twin " and her " better half "—or, rather, half of her head and three-quarters of the head of her husband, Mr. John Barran. Mrs. John Barran and the Hon. Margaret Hore-Ruthven are daughters of General Lord Ruthven, and were famous for their inseparability, their charm, and the fact that they always dressed alike. They were divided by the marriage of the Hon. Alison Hore-Ruthven to Mr. John Barran, eldest son of Sir John Barran, Bt., which took place in March last.

PHOTOGRAPH BY YEVONDE, EXCLUSIVE TO " THE SKETCH."

Yva
(Else Ernestine Neuländer-Simon)
1900, Germany–1942, Poland

Else Ernestine Neuländer-Simon, known by the pseudonym Yva, was a fashion photographer and portraitist who enjoyed great success in Berlin during the inter-war period. Her studio, which opened in 1925, employed up to ten assistants, including the future photographer Helmut Newton. Her images were published in a number of illustrated magazines and she was given several commissions for advertising work. She took a number of nudes and experimented with multiple exposures. Her photographs emphasize the silhouette of the modern woman and take a bold and playful attitude to erotic and androgynous ambiguity.

As she was Jewish, the rise to power of the Nazi regime led to growing restrictions from 1933 onwards, and she was unable to pursue her profession. In 1938, she decided to give it up and work for the radiology department of the Jewish Hospital. In 1942, she and her husband were deported and they were both killed in a Polish concentration camp.

38. Untitled, 1929.

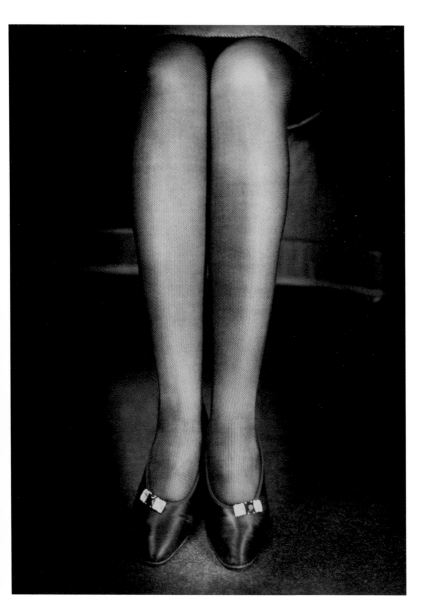

Berenice Abbott
1898–1991, USA

Berenice Abbott studied art in the avant-garde circles of New York before moving to Paris in 1921 to study sculpture. She trained in photography under Man Ray, a compatriot who was also living in the French capital, and in 1926 she opened her own studio where she took portraits of artists and intellectuals.

On her return to New York in 1929, she promoted the work of French photographer Eugène Atget, who had recorded the transformations that had taken place in Paris at the turn of the century and some of whose works she had acquired. She then embarked on a huge project to record the changes that were transforming New York City, with the support of the Museum of the City of New York, which exhibited her work in the 1930s, and the Federal Art Project, a US national programme to fund the visual arts. This project, entitled *Changing New York*, shows how old buildings and new structures existed side by side and includes industrial areas and the city harbour, combining overall views with fragmented details. A team of researchers compiled the documentation explaining the images, based around maps, conversations and press cuttings. The complete work was published as a book in 1939.

Abbott went on to produce photographs for the Massachusetts Institute of Technology (MIT), using abstract compositions to illustrate the principles of mechanics and optics. During her career, she patented designs for photographic equipment, published two handbooks on photography and taught at the New School for Social Research in New York (1934–58).

39. Self-portrait, *c*. 1930.

Gertrud Arndt

1903, Poland–2000, Germany

Gertrud Hantschk studied architecture and then turned to
photography in order to take pictures of local buildings. She also
trained in drawing, graphic art and art history before enrolling at
the Bauhaus in 1923. There she studied under László Moholy-Nagy
and worked in the weaving workshop. In 1927, she married architect
and fellow Bauhaus student Alfred Arndt. She then specialized in
architectural photography on behalf of her husband's architectural
practice. In 1929, the couple returned to the Bauhaus where Hannes
Meyer had invited her husband to teach.

   During this period, Gertrud Arndt photographed still lifes,
portraits of her friends and the series for which she is best known,
performative self-portraits. In these images, she appears masked
or veiled, an embodiment of a provocative female stereotype,
looking straight at the lens and partially revealing her body. Her
images, ranging from the absurd to the unsettling and playful,
form an original contribution to the history of the photographic
self-portrait.

40. Masked portrait no. 16, Dessau, Germany, 1930.

Marianne Brandt

1893–1983, Germany

After studying painting and sculpture, Marianne Brandt produced Expressionist work before enrolling at the Bauhaus in 1924. She trained in the metal workshop, of which she later became director. Here she created artisanal objects with stark forms, imprinting her signature on what was traditionally a male-dominated field. She went on to design lamps, which were manufactured on an industrial scale, and joined a metal workshop as a designer, before eventually devoting herself to teaching. An important member of the Bauhaus movement, she created classic designs, especially her tea services, some of which were later reissued by the Italian design company Alessi.

Her photographic work, rediscovered much later, includes still lifes, self-portraits and photomontages. The latter, which were based on press cuttings, take a critical look at the growth of technology and the situation of women in the inter-war period.

41. With All Ten Fingers, 1930.

Annelise Kretschmer

1903–87, Germany

After studying drawing and bookbinding, Annelise Silberbach
learned the techniques of photography, her field of choice,
by working in portrait studios. She opened her own studio in
Dortmund in the late 1920s. In 1928, she married the sculptor
Sigmund Kretschmer. Inspired by the experimental work of the
New Photography movement, she took part in the influential
exhibition 'Film und Foto' in 1929. She photographed well-known
figures from the art world, as well as fishermen and workers. In the
late 1930s, she produced a series of photographs of farmworkers'
children, depicting them as fully rounded people at a time when
minors did not have an acknowledged status.

Her portraits are characterized by a frontal approach, innovative
framing that sometimes cropped off part of the subject, and a
quest for psychological intensity, emphasizing the subject's gaze
and gestures. Her photographs of women helped to establish the
dynamic concept of the 'New Woman'.

42. Unknown woman, 1930.

Grit Kallin-Fischer

1897, Germany–1973, USA

Grit Kallin studied painting in Leipzig before enrolling at the
Bauhaus in 1926. She studied under the painters Paul Klee and
Wassily Kandinsky, experimenting with the principles of abstraction.
She also worked in the Bauhaus stage design studio, which was
where she first began to explore photography. She moved to Berlin
in 1928, where she worked for the press. After her marriage in 1934
to Edward L. Fischer, an American and fellow Bauhaus student,
she moved to New York and then to Pennsylvania, where she
continued her artistic work.

Kallin-Fischer took close-up portraits, experimenting with
lighting to create an unusual and dramatic atmosphere. Her still
lifes and abstract works are based around isolated geometric forms,
echoing the experimental work of the Bauhaus.

43. Freddo Bartolucci, *c.* 1930–31.

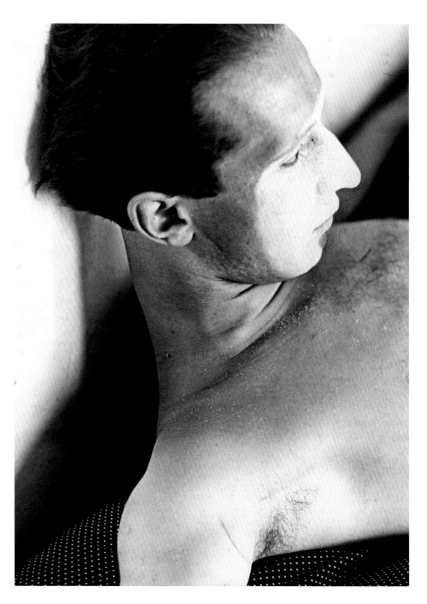

Clara E. Sipprell

1885, Canada–1975, USA

Clara E. Sipprell grew up in Canada and then moved to Buffalo, New York, with her family. She trained in the photography studio of her older brother, where she worked for ten years. Subsequently she moved to New York where she opened her own studio and took portraits of figures from the art world. Refusing to use artificial lighting or to crop her images, she only worked in natural light and constructed her compositions at the moment she took her photographs. Influenced by Pictorialism, she photographed her models' faces in soft focus and tried to emphasize each sitter's personality.

Although best known for her portraits, she also took still lifes and landscape photographs, remaining faithful to the Pictorialist style. In the 1920s, she travelled to Russia, Yugoslavia and Sweden, where she photographed members of the Swedish royal family; she later visited Spain, Portugal, Italy, Greece, Japan, the UK and France. She compiled a collection of her best work that was exhibited in 1960 at Syracuse University, which now holds her archives.

44. Santa Fe, New Mexico, 1930–40.

Liselotte Grschebina
1908, Germany–1994, Israel

After studying art in Hamburg, Liselotte Grschebina set up the
Bilfoto studio in 1932, specializing in child photography. As she was
of Jewish origin, she was forced to close her studio in 1933 when
the Nazis came to power. She settled in Tel Aviv in 1934, where she
spent two years running the Ishon studio with her friend Ellen
Auerbach. From 1934 to 1947, she was an official photographer
for the Women's International Zionist Organization (WIZO).
She recorded kibbutz life, industry, and the railway networks that
were being built in the region. Her approach was influenced by
the principles of the New Vision movement and the European
avant-garde, under whom she had trained. Her work is characterized
by the use of unusual angles and the effects of perspective, light and
shade, resulting in geometric compositions. She was also known for
her theatre photography, in which she focused on masks, costumes
and stage sets.

In 1939, she co-founded the Palestine Professional
Photographers' Association. Her archives, comprising some
1,800 images, are now preserved at the Israel Museum in Jerusalem.

45. Masks, *c.* 1930.

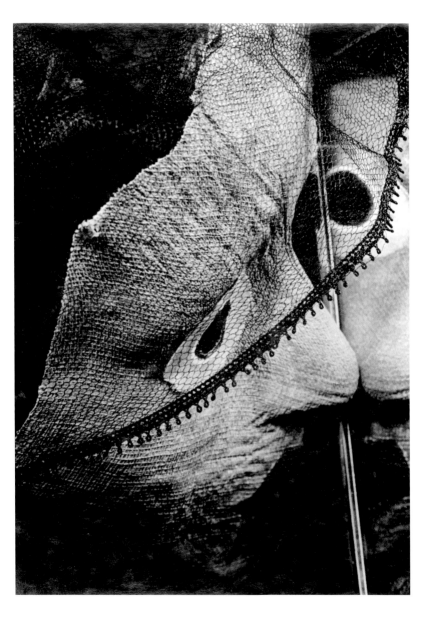

Olga Spolarich
1895, Hungary–1969, Austria

Born in Budapest, Olga Spolarich married Ardoján Wlassics in Vienna in 1920. In around 1924, the couple opened the Manassé studio, specializing in portraits of women. Spolarich was in charge of decor, staging and shooting, while her husband concentrated on retouching. Clients flocked to the studio, admiring the couple's ability to create attractive and elegant images that showed them at their most glamorous. This success led them to open another studio in Bucharest, followed by one in Berlin, catering for a clientele from the world of stage and screen. At the end of the 1930s, they gave up the name Manassé and henceforth Spolarich worked under the name Olga Wlassics. She moved to Berlin in 1940, before returning to Austria to found the Foto Wlassics studio in 1948. After the death of her first husband, she married the photographer Hans Rothen. She exhibited at the Wiener Kunsthalle in the late 1950s.

Spolarich, sometimes known as Solarics, is best known for the erotic photographs in a Surrealist style she created in around 1930. Her photomontages feature nude bodies in unusual settings. She often focused on differences of scale, as in her photograph of a woman wearing nothing but shoes, a mask and long black gloves, posing in front of a gigantic fan. Several compositions feature the motif of decapitated male heads, perhaps a disturbing or morbid allusion to multiple lovers.

46. Actress Lil Dagover in a publicity shot for
Madame Bluebeard by Conrad Wiene, *c*. 1930.

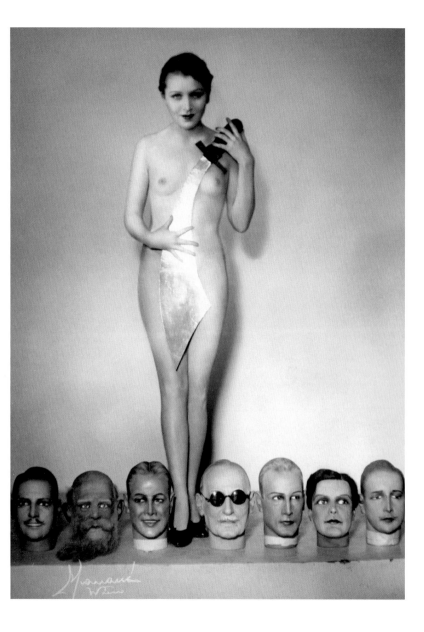

Wynn Richards
1888–1960, USA

After training as a Pictorialist photographer at the Clarence H.
White School of Photography in New York, Martha Wynn Richards
returned to her home town in Mississippi in 1919 and opened a
studio. When she practised her art by having a local teacher pose
for her in the nude, this caused a huge scandal. She then decided to
leave her husband and move to New York, where she shot fashion
photographs and interiors for *Vogue* between 1922 and 1924. As the
magazine evolved, she abandoned the Pictorialist style in favour of
a more direct approach, emphasizing more boyish silhouettes. She
signed her images 'Wynn Richards', omitting her first name Martha
and her nickname Matsy so as not to be stigmatized by her gender.

   She then opened a studio in Chicago with her friend Betty
Frear, before returning to New York in 1928 to specialize in
fashion, portraiture and advertising. She helped to found a fashion
photography group in New York and encouraged young women to
pursue this career. In 1934, her fashion photographs were exhibited
at the Julien Levy Gallery. She then married the British naval officer
Herbert Taylor, who managed her studio until his death in 1947.
At the end of her life, she returned to her home town and opened
her last studio, taking portraits of her grandchildren and local
young people. Wynn Richards was one of the first female fashion
photographers and was committed to helping other women to join
the profession.

47. Before & After, *c.* 1932.

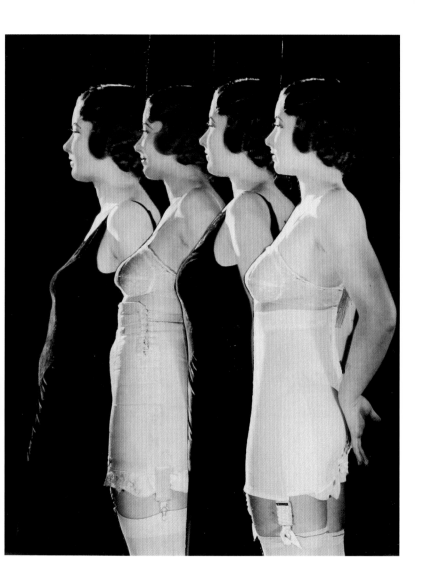

Ellen Auerbach
1906, Germany–2004, USA

After studying art, Ellen Rosenberg went to Berlin in 1929 to
study photography in the studio of Walter Peterhans, where she
met and became close friends with Grete Stern. Together they
opened a studio specializing in portraits, fashion photography and
advertising, which they named 'ringl + pit' after their childhood
nicknames, signing their images jointly. At that time, advertising
was a flourishing field and offered great scope for experimentation.
They created unusual compositions using objects and mannequins,
making a witty contribution to the dynamic ideal of the 'New
Woman'. Ellen also turned to cinema, making two short films,
one experimental and one narrative.

When Hitler came to power in 1933, the two photographers,
both of Jewish origin, decided to leave. Ellen went to Palestine
where she made a film on the growth of Tel Aviv. Together with
her companion and future husband Walter Auerbach, she set up
a studio specializing in portraits of children. In 1936, they went
to London to meet up again with Grete Stern, before moving to
Philadelphia, where Ellen photographed the Lessing-Rosenwald art
collection, and then to New York in 1940. She continued to travel
until the 1960s, concentrating on landscapes, portraits and street
photography. At the age of sixty, she gave up photography to work
with children with learning difficulties.

48. Advertisement for Komol hair dye, ringl + pit, 1932.

Laura Gilpin

1891–1979, USA

Born in Colorado, Laura Gilpin trained at the Clarence H. White photography school in New York from 1916 to 1918, adopting the Pictorialist style that predominated at the time. She returned to her native region to work as a portrait photographer and take on commissions for architectural photography, but is best known for her photographs of Native Americans. In 1941, she published a book on the Pueblo Indians, followed in 1951 by a work on the Navajo people.

Gilpin is also famous for her landscapes of the American Southwest, challenging the male tradition of explorer photographers. Her work stands out from that of her predecessors through her historical approach to landscape. She highlights the relationship between human activities and the environment and the way that Native American peoples inhabited their landscapes, shaped by archaeological remains and ancient trails. This investigation of the past invests her carefully crafted images with a very personal intensity.

49. Steps of El Castillo, Chichén Itzá, Mexico, 1932.

Kata Kálmán
1909–78, Hungary

Kata Kálmán studied at the Alice Madzsar School of Dance, where she trained in the Mesendieck system of physiotherapy and gymnastics and met the photographer Kata Sugár. In 1929, she married the art theorist Iván Hevesy, who encouraged her to take up photography. Influenced by the rigorous style of New Objectivity, she took an approach that was both sociological and empathetic and made portraits of farmers, the unemployed and children. Her best-known photograph, taken in Budapest in 1931, is an image of a four-year-old child in ragged clothes, devouring a slice of bread, with a gaze that is direct and unsettling.

She published several books: *Tiborc* (1937), *Szemtöl szembe* (1940) and *Tiborc új arca* (1955), a collection of her images of rural life. She also took portraits of major figures from the Hungarian cultural world, including the composer Béla Bartók. She edited and played a major role in the creation of a series of photography books published by the Corvina publishing house, the last of which, released after her death, was devoted to her own work.

50. Ernö Weisz, 23-year-old factory worker, Budapest, 1932.

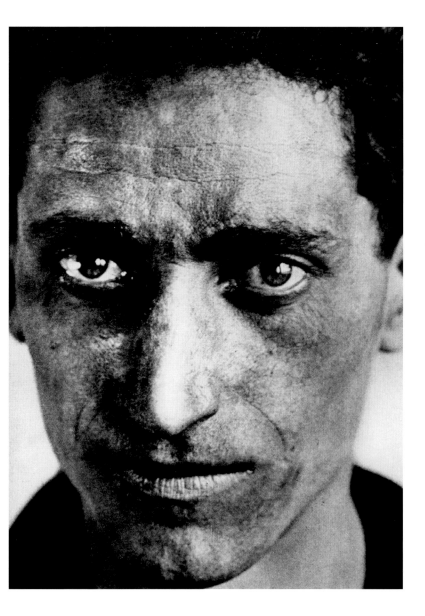

Ergy Landau
1896, Hungary–1967, France

Born into a prosperous family in Budapest, Ergy Landau trained in photography in Vienna and Berlin before returning to Hungary and opening her own studio. She frequented avant-garde artistic circles and was inspired by the experiments of the New Vision movement. She was forced to leave Hungary in 1923 because of the unstable political situation and took refuge in Paris, where she befriended other Hungarian émigrés including Brassaï and André Kertész. Her work was shown in several exhibitions, including 'Film und Foto' in 1929, and her reputation began to grow.

Her high-angle view of the railway lines at the Gare Saint-Lazare, highlighting the sinuous curves of the tracks, reflects her love of avant-garde artistic innovation. She is also known for her advertising work, portraits of writers and photographs of children, published via the Rapho agency in books and illustrated magazines such as *VU*. She travelled to China and, together with the writer Pierre Gascar, published *Aujourd'hui la Chine* in 1955. She illustrated two books for children: *Le Petit Chat*, with the writer Maurice Genevoix, and *Horoldamba*, a picture book about a Mongolian boy. She experimented with nudes, photographing women in the intimate settings of their daily lives, even depicting prosaic activities such as leg-shaving. Throughout her career, Ergy Landau followed the photographic trends of her time, from her Pictorialist beginnings to her humanist work, making a name for herself on the Parisian art scene.

51. Gare Saint-Lazare, Paris, 1932.

Edith Tudor-Hart

1908, Austria–1973, UK

Born in Vienna, Edith Tudor-Hart trained in photography at the Bauhaus in Dessau and was a committed supporter of the Communist Party. She became known for her photographs of the working classes and the hardships of the unemployed in her native city. Under threat because of her political activism and Jewish origins, she fled to the UK in 1933 with her husband, an English doctor, and concentrated on documentary photography. She worked mainly for the Communist Party and photographed workers in London and South Wales.

Although a recognized photographer, she in fact led a double life as a spy for the Soviet Union. In particular, she was involved in the recruitment of Kim Philby, a member of the famous Cambridge spy ring and a double agent for the British secret service who also worked for the KGB. In 2015, Austrian writer Peter Stephan Jungk, a distant relative of Edith Tudor-Hart, published a biography describing her exceptional life.

52. Unemployed Workers' Demonstration, Vienna, 1932.

Wanda Wulz

1903, Austria–1984, Italy

Wanda Wulz worked as an assistant and model in her family's photographic studio, founded in 1868 by her grandfather in their native town of Trieste. In 1928, she and her sister Marion took over the reins of the studio, which had become a meeting place for members of the local artistic scene. She experimented with the technique of photomontage and embraced the innovations of the Futurist movement, which she joined in 1931 after meeting its founder, the writer Filippo Marinetti. Interested in depicting motion and speed, she was inspired by the work of filmmaker and photographer Anton Giulio Bragaglia, a member of the Futurists and pioneer of photodynamism, a technique that used long exposures to capture the trails of light made by bodies in motion.

The double-exposure image made up of a self-portrait superimposed with the image of a cat is Wulz's most famous work. With its staring eyes, half human and half animal, it is both strange and playful, suggesting a masked ball or perhaps a dream.

53. Io + Gatto (Me + Cat), 1932.

Sonya Noskowiak

1900, Germany–1975, USA

Born in Leipzig, Sonya Noskowiak grew up in Chile before her
family moved to California in 1915. She trained as a secretary and
then became an assistant in Johan Hagemeyer's studio. Through him,
she met the photographer Edward Weston, becoming his companion
and model from 1929 to 1935. She took photographs of modern
urban architecture and close-ups of natural motifs, such as the petals
of a flower, the contours of a plant, or marks left on sand and rocks.
Verging on abstraction, these geometric compositions followed the
lines of Weston's work and the principles of Group f/64, of which
she was a member.

After separating from Weston, she opened her own portrait
studio in San Francisco and took on an assignment for the Federal
Art Project. Rather than capturing isolated details or objects, she
shot broader views, reflecting her interest in the social and human
context of her landscapes. Her work, now conserved by the Center
for Creative Photography in Tucson, Arizona, was a key contribution
to the avant-garde movements of the West Coast of the USA.

54. Sand pattern, 1932.

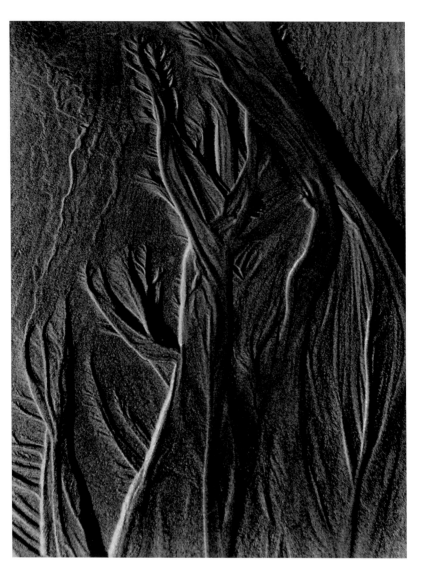

Lotte Jacobi

1896, Germany–1990, USA

After studying literature and art history Lotte Jacobi (born Johanna Alexandre Jacobi) trained as a photographer, continuing a family tradition that dated back to her great-grandfather. She ran her father's studio in Berlin from 1927 to 1935 and took portraits of eminent figures from intellectual and artistic life, including László Moholy-Nagy.

Of Jewish origin and affiliated with left-wing political circles, with the rise of Nazism she fled to New York, where she ran her own studio until 1955. She photographed major cultural, political and scientific figures, including Albert Einstein, who was a family friend.

In the 1950s, she moved to New Hampshire where she set up a studio gallery and experimented with landscapes and abstract images, created by manipulating photographic paper. She also became involved in Democratic Party politics. The portraits of Lotte Jacobi serve as valuable records of European and American intellectual life in the second quarter of the 20th century.

55. Anton Walbrook, actor, Berlin, 1933.

Gertrude Fehr

1895, Germany–1996, Switzerland

After training in Munich, Gertrude Fehr opened a studio specializing in theatre photography and portraits. Of Jewish origin, she was obliged to leave Germany and subsequently set up a studio in Paris in 1933. Together with her husband, the Swiss painter Jules Fehr, she opened the Publiphot school, which offered an original approach to the medium, inspired by the innovations of the New Photography movement. She primarily taught advertising photography, which she regarded as an entirely valid form of artistic expression. She also experimented with nudes, portraits, and manipulation techniques such as photomontage and solarization. She fled to Switzerland in 1939 and opened a new school in Lausanne, at a time when photographic training was still rare. Inspired by her success, she wanted to enlarge her school but met with opposition from the Swiss Union of Photographers and had to abandon the project. In 1945, her school was integrated into the École des Arts et Métiers in Vevey.

Fehr engaged in avant-garde experimentation and was notable for teaching generations of photographers as well as publishing her own work in magazines and photography journals. Her archives are now preserved by the Musée de l'Élysée in Lausanne.

56. Composition, *c.* 1935.

Marjorie Content
1895–1984, USA

Born into a prosperous family, Marjorie Content was interested in the radical thought and avant-garde literary work of the early 20th century. She married the poet Harold Loeb and between 1919 and 1921 she was one of the directors of The Sunwise Turn, a bookshop founded and financed by women, which specialized in contemporary literature. On the death of her second husband, she moved to New York and in 1926 she turned to photography, with the support of Alfred Stieglitz, founder of the Photo-Secession. She travelled frequently around the southwestern United States, paying regular visits to her friend, the painter Georgia O'Keeffe, with whom she went to Bermuda in 1933.

In 1934, she met the writer Jean Toomer, a member of the Harlem Renaissance movement, who went on to become her fourth husband. She was given a brief assignment from the Bureau of Indian Affairs to record the lives of Native Americans. From 1935 onwards, she lived on a farm in Pennsylvania and eventually gave up photography. Her archives, which include her correspondence with members of the artistic and literary circles of the time, are conserved by Yale University.

57. Laundry, New York, 1935.

Eudora Welty

1909–2001, USA

Eudora Welty was a distinguished American fiction writer. She studied advertising before working for a radio station and for the Federal Agency of the Works Progress Administration, as well as writing for *The Commercial Appeal*, a Memphis newspaper. She also experimented with photography, recording the difficulties faced by workers during the Great Depression, as well as African American communities. Her photographic work, exhibited in New York in 1936 and 1937, is marked by her empathy, and echoes the characters and themes featured in her books.

Her literary career, for which she won a number of prizes, eventually took over from photography. She became best known for her analysis of the racial problems and culture of the American South. Her short stories and novels were written in a realist style, strong on detail and dialogue, although she took inspiration from legends and myths. Books on her photographic work were published in 1971 (*One Time, One Place*) and again in 1989, 2000 and 2009.

58. Oseola McCarty, philanthropist, Hinds County, Mississippi, 1935.

Dora Maar
1907–97, France

Henriette Theodora Markovitch grew up in Argentina before returning to her city of birth, Paris, in 1926, where she studied painting and photography. She adopted the name Dora Maar, shared a studio with Brassaï and befriended Emmanuel Sougez. She produced photograms and still lifes, influenced by Modernist experiments, together with erotic nudes, advertising work, portraits, fashion photographs and street photography, in particular during her trip to Spain in 1934. She entered into a relationship with the filmmaker Louis Chavance and then with the writer Georges Bataille, and frequented avant-garde circles. During this period, she created original photomontages that reflect a fascination with the strange and the erotic that was typical of the Surrealists, to whose exhibitions she contributed work in 1934 and 1937.

She became Picasso's muse and companion in 1935. They created photograms together before she returned to painting. Her portrait paintings were inspired by Cubism and her still lifes by the unusual angles favoured by the members of the New Photography movement. When she and Picasso separated in 1946, she suffered from depression and became a patient of the psychoanalyst Jacques Lacan. She then lived alone and concentrated on making paintings and prints of the landscapes of Provence, only returning briefly to photography in the 1980s.

'Silence' is a photomontage that reflects her bold photographic work of the mid-1930s, blurring the limits between the unconscious and the imaginary by means of distorted perspectives that create a nightmarish effect.

59. Silence, 1935.

Margaret Bourke-White

1904–71, USA

Margaret Bourke-White trained as a photographer at the Clarence H. White school in New York, while also studying zoology. She opened her first studio in her apartment in Cleveland, Ohio, gaining a reputation for her photographs of buildings and industry. In 1929, the press mogul Henry Luce offered her a full-time job with *Fortune* magazine. In 1936, he launched the famous weekly magazine *Life*, which featured a photograph by Bourke-White on the cover of the first issue. This majestic view of the construction of Fort Peck Dam was a tribute to innovation and progress. Bourke-White subsequently became a photojournalist for *Life*, working in Germany, the Soviet Union and the USA. She published several illustrated books with the writer Erskine Caldwell, to whom she was married from 1939 to 1942.

She covered the Second World War for *Life*, flying in fighter planes to record the aerial bombardments in North Africa, before photographing the Italian campaign, the siege of Moscow and the liberation of the concentration camps. She went on to photograph the partition of India and Pakistan and the Korean War. Her experience in the field gained her a reputation as a war reporter that was to prove an inspiration to her female contemporaries.

60. Fort Peck Dam, Montana, 1936.

Dorothea Lange

1895–1965, USA

Dorothea Lange studied photography at Columbia University in New York before opening a portrait studio in San Francisco in 1918. During the 1930s, she recorded the hardships of the unemployed, whose numbers had increased massively in the wake of the Wall Street crash of 1929. She took part in the major photography project run by the Farm Security Administration (FSA), aimed at showing the living and working conditions in rural communities and small towns hit by the crisis. In Nipomo, California, she photographed Florence Owens Thompson, a farm worker, with her children. One of the shots, a simple, tightly framed portrait focusing on Thompson's face, inspired huge sympathy and was to become an iconic image of the Great Depression.

In 1949, Lange published a selection of her work in the book *An American Exodus: A Record of Human Erosion*, accompanied by a text written by her husband, Paul Schuster Taylor, a professor of agricultural economics at the University of California, Berkeley. In 1942, she recorded the mass evacuation of Americans of Japanese origin to detention camps, following the attack on Pearl Harbor. After the war, she produced photo-essays for *Life* magazine. In 1953–54, she assisted Edward Steichen, photographer and curator at the Museum of Modern Art (MoMA), by recruiting photographers to take part in 'The Family of Man', a major exhibition that served as a manifesto of humanism in photography. She went on to travel the world, visiting South America, the Middle East and South Asia. In 1965, she helped to curate a retrospective of her work at MoMA, which opened soon after her death.

61. Migrant Mother (Florence Owens Thompson), Nipomo, California, 1936.

Picture Credits

1. Anna Atkins: © Photo12 / Alamy
2. Mary Dillwyn: © Mary Dillwyn's Llysdinam Album / The National Library of Wales, Aberystwyth
3. Virginia Oldoïni, Countess of Castiglione: © Photo-Re-Pubblic / Leemage
4. Lady Clementina Hawarden: © Victoria & Albert Museum, London
5. Julia Margaret Cameron: © SSPL / Leemage
6. Frances Benjamin Johnston: © Bridgeman Images
7. Eveleen Myers: © National Portrait Gallery, London
8. Alice Austen: © Collection of Historic Richmond Town, New York
9. Hannah Maynard: © Royal British Columbia Museum, Victoria, Canada / Courtesy of the Royal BC Museum and Archives / Bridgeman Images
10. Belle Johnson: © Courtesy of the Massillon Museum, Ohio
11. Zaida Ben-Yúsuf: © Granger / Bridgeman Images
12. Gertrude Käsebier © GraphicaArtis / Bridgeman Images
13. Jessie Tarbox Beals: © Museum of the City of New York
14. Alice Boughton: © Photo12 / Alamy
15. Anne Brigman: © / RMN-Grand Palais (Musée d'Orsay) / Jean-Gilles Berizzi
16. Minya Diez-Dührkoop: © Age Fotostock
17. Adelaide Hanscom: © Photo12 / Alamy
18. Olive Edis: © National Portrait Gallery, London
19. Claude Cahun: © Jersey Heritage Trust, UK / Bridgeman Images
20. Charlotte Rudolph: © Adagp, Paris, 2020
21. Margrethe Mather: © The J. Paul Getty Museum, Los Angeles
22. Dora Kallmus (Madame d'Ora): © Madame d'Ora / Imagno / Roger-Viollet
23. Tina Modotti: © QuintLox / Leemage
24. Lucia Moholy: © The Metropolitan Museum of Art, Dist. RMN-Grand Palais / image of the MMA; © Adagp, Paris, 2020
25. Trude Fleischmann: © The J. Paul Getty Museum, Los Angeles
26. Germaine Krull: © Centre Pompidou, MNAM-CCI, Dist. RMN-Grand Palais / Georges Meguerditchian; © Museum Folkwang, Essen
27. Lotte Beese: © Estate of Lotte Beese / The J. Paul Getty Museum, Los Angeles
28. Marta Astfalck-Vietz © Berlinische Galerie / Anja Elisabeth Witte; © Adagp, Paris, 2020
29. Rogi André (Rosa Klein): © Bibliothèque Nationale de France
30. Aenne Biermann: © Museum Folkwang Essen / Artothek / La Collection
31. Florence Henri: © Galleria Martini & Ronchetti, Genova; courtesy Archives Florence Henri
32. Imogen Cunningham: © Imogen Cunningham Trust, 2020